SandCastle

Dollars & Cents

# A Penny = 1¢

10900

Carey Molter

Consulting Editor, Monica Marx, M.A./Reading Specialist

ABDO
Publishing Company

White Heath School
300 High St.
White Heath, IL 61884

Published by SandCastle™, an imprint of ABDO Publishing Company, 4940 Viking Drive, Edina, Minnesota 55435.

Credits
Edited by: Pam Price
Curriculum Coordinator: Nancy Tuminelly
Cover and Interior Design and Production: Mighty Media
Photo Credits: AbleStock, Comstock, Eyewire Images, PhotoDisc, Rubberball

Library of Congress Cataloging-in-Publication Data

Molter, Carey, 1973-
    A penny = 1¢ / Carey Molter.
      p. cm. -- (Dollars & cents)
    Includes index.
    Summary: Explains what a penny is, how many pennies there are in a dollar, and how many are needed to purchase different items.
    ISBN 1-57765-888-4
    1. Money--Juvenile literature. [1. Money.] I. Title: Penny equals one cent. II. Title. III. Series

HG221.5 .M657 2002
332.4'973--dc21

                                                                    2002071186

SandCastle™ books are created by a professional team of educators, reading specialists, and content developers around five essential components that include phonemic awareness, phonics, vocabulary, text comprehension, and fluency. All books are written, reviewed, and leveled for guided reading, early intervention reading, and Accelerated Reader® programs and designed for use in shared, guided, and independent reading and writing activities to support a balanced approach to literacy instruction.

# Let Us Know

After reading the book, SandCastle would like you to tell us your stories about reading. What is your favorite page? Was there something hard that you needed help with? Share the ups and downs of learning to read. We want to hear from you! To get posted on the ABDO Publishing Company Web site, send us email at:

**sandcastle@abdopub.com**

**SandCastle Level: Beginning**

This is a penny.

A penny is a coin.

One penny is the same as one cent.

This is how to write one cent.

1¢

Five pennies is the same as one nickel.

Ten pennies is the same
as one dime.

**Twenty-five** pennies
is the same as one quarter.

One gumdrop costs 1¢.

That is one penny.

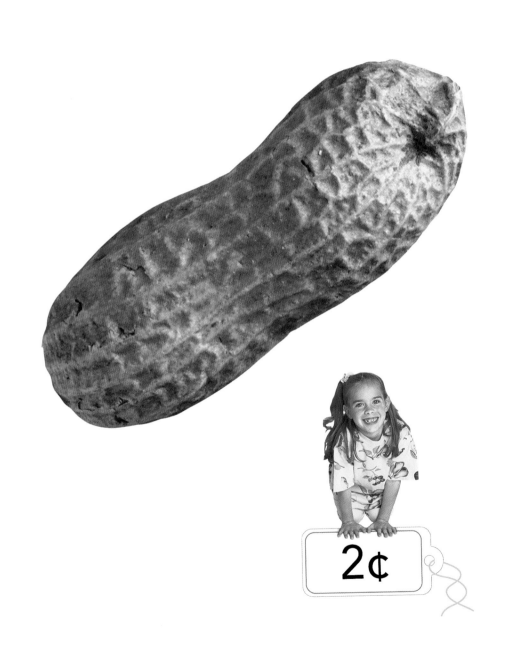

2¢

This peanut costs 2¢.

That is two pennies.

This piece of paper
costs 3¢.

That is three pennies.

This stamp costs 4¢.

How many pennies is that?

(four)

# Picture Index

dime, p. 11

penny, pp. 3, 5, 7, 15

nickel, p. 9

quarter, p. 13

# More about the Penny

President Abraham Lincoln

Year the coin was made

Where the coin was made. The letter *D* means it came from Denver, Colorado

*E pluribus unum* means one out of many

Smooth edges

The Lincoln Memorial

# About SandCastle™

A professional team of educators, reading specialists, and content developers created the SandCastle™ series to support young readers as they develop reading skills and strategies and increase their general knowledge. The SandCastle™ series has four levels that correspond to early literacy development in young children. The levels are provided to help teachers and parents select the appropriate books for young readers.

**Emerging Readers**
(no flags)

**Beginning Readers**
(1 flag)

**Transitional Readers**
(2 flags)

**Fluent Readers**
(3 flags)

These levels are meant only as a guide. All levels are subject to change.

To see a complete list of SandCastle™ books and other nonfiction titles from ABDO Publishing Company, visit **www.abdopub.com** or contact us at:

4940 Viking Drive, Edina, Minnesota 55435 • 1-800-800-1312 • fax: 1-952-831-1632